CW00674506

Stretford

in old picture postcards

selected and compiled by
Stretford Local History Society

European Library – Zaltbommel/Netherlands

Acknowledgements:
We would like to thank Trafford Leisure Services for permission to use library photographs and postcards in the compilation of this volume.

Further reading:
History of Stretford, S. Massey, 1976.
The Dukes Cut, G. Wheat, 1977.
Manchester Tramways, I. Yeardsley/P. Groves, 1988.
Old Stretford, J.E. Bailey, 1985.
Old Stretford, Sir Bosdin Leech, 1910.
Stretford in times past, M. Redhead, 1979.
Stretford People & Places, Stretford Local History, 1985.
Stretford, the changing scene, Stretford Local History.

GB ISBN 90 288 5513 0 / CIP

INTRODUCTION

Rhubarb, pork and blackpuddings were the major products of Stretford in the eighteenth and nineteenth century. The development of the Bridgewater Canal and the Manchester South Junction and Altrincham Railway at a later date were important in the development of Stretford as a market garden for Manchester and the rapidly expanding industrial areas of South Lancashire.

From the opening of the Manchester Ship Canal in 1894 and the subsequent development of Trafford Park as an industrial estate from 1900 onwards, it was inevitable that Stretford's rural way of life would eventually have to give way to the march of the twentieth century.

Well-known manufacturing names took their place in Trafford Park; Westinghouse (Metro's), now G.E.C., in 1899; Ford Motors in 1911 and many others. The Great War served to consolidate the concerns of those already there and attracted others either in a primary or sub-contracting role.

The Docks became a hive of activity, with ships from all over the world loading and unloading and railways increased accordingly. As if in anticipation of this growth, Stretford Urban District Council came into being in 1894. The new industries would need electricity, gas, water and other amenities. Over the next twenty years the Stretford U.D.C. provided these necessities. There was one other essential element in the growth of the area and that was labour. Many thousands of people were needed to man the expansion of industry and services and this meant an increase in the provision of housing.

Gradually, from 1910 onwards, the separate communities of Old Trafford and Stretford, once surrounded by fields and farms, began to be linked by housing development. First growth was concentrated along the main roads. Later the density of housing increased as in the Gorse Hill area. Thus Stretford, by the start of the 1920s, had, as it were, assimilated the Ship Canal complex and the Trafford Park Estate and was ready to take off. In the next twenty years, despite the depression and trade slumps, the area was to assume its present form.

Many changes have taken place since the 1930s. Property has been demolished for road widening and the Arndale Centre has replaced the old King Street. The Trafford Park area has been transformed in recent years and cinemas have been demolished or converted to other uses. These changes are inevitable and it is hoped that the photographs will enable readers to imagine familiar areas as they evolved between the late 1800s and the 1930s.

Hearty Greetings to the OLD BOYS from the FIRST LONGFORDS. May the Welcome PEACE bring an early Home-Coming.

XMAS 1918.

"THE RANCHE", LONGFORD PARK, STRETFORD. MANCHESTER

1. *The 1st Longford Scout Troop.* The 1st Longford Scout Troop was started by Mr. W.E. Gregson in 1908 at the Union Church in Edge Lane. The following year the first camp was pitched in Lime Road. A few years later the troop was given the use of the shippon in Longford Park, which was renamed 'The Ranche', refurbishing the building themselves with funds raised by efforts such as bazaars. In 1918 the Stretford Division comprising seven troops was formed. At that time the entire uniform of hat, scarf, shirt, shorts, belt, stockings, haversack, staff and shoulder knot cost 17/6 (87.5p) and the cost of entering for a badge was one penny per head. Scoutmasters were advised 'to insist on all scouts having their hair cut within at least seven days before camp'. 1st Longford Troop were represented at the World Jamboree in Birkenhead in 1929.

2. *The Church Brass Band*. Stretford like many other towns in the 1800s supported much musical activity. The earliest band formed was the 'Ould Band'. Later in 1877 the Church Band was formed and in 1879 the Village Band. The picture shows the Church Band about 1890. Note the sartorial elegance of the players!

3. *Stretford's Old Prize Band.* Stretford's Old Prize Band is shown here in July 1927 at a concert in the Civic Theatre, celebrating the band's fiftieth anniversary. Earlier called the 'Church Band', it was commonly called 'Rogerson's' − the conductor, chairman, treasurer and three bandsmen bearing that name. The four-manual organ had been installed by Mrs. Rylands. It had a small, town-gas engined pump, later changed to an electric pump. The connection between the band and the organ is that Nellie, sister of bandsman Joe Hampson, married Reg Tither, manager of Jardine's of Old Trafford, who made the organ.

4. *The cenotaph.* In 1919 Stretford Council organised a public appeal for subscriptions for a War Memorial. More than £9,000 was raised. £2,000 was set aside for a cenotaph at Gorse Hill on land provided by the De Trafford Trustees. On Saturday, 25th August 1923, the cenotaph was unveiled by the Earl of Derby. A wreath was laid by Lt. Harry Coverdale, a Stretford man, who won a V.C. in the war, on behalf of the ex-service men of Stretford. 580 Stretford service men were killed in the First World War.

5. *Eye Platt Bridge.* The river Mersey originally wandered wide and shallow between the Old Cock Hotel and Sale and this presented many problems. The nature of these problems is shown by the name Eye Platt, 'Eye' referring to land surrounded by water and 'Platt' to a foot bridge. The level of the road was raised to above the flood level and the four arches constructed to allow flood water to pass along a channel built for this purpose. The arches were known as Eye Platt Bridge. Further banking made this channel unnecessary and it was filled-in by controlled tipping, the land being used for recreational purposes.

6. *Cut Hole Bridge*. This bridge on Hawthorn Lane carries the Bridgewater Canal and was constructed especially to cope with flood water from the river Mersey.

7. *Chapel Lane.* This view down Chapel Lane towards Barton Road dates from the mid-1920s. Temperance Vine, on the right-hand side, was built by John Fallows, a potato merchant. He occupied the house on the extreme right. Eight houses faced Chapel Lane, while another five were down an entry by the gas lamp, later becoming 53-61 Church Street. The hedge on the left bounded Cobb Hall Farm and is the sight of 9-17 Chapel Lane which extends from Woodland Terrace to Cobb Hall Road, now the entrance to Stretford House. In the centre, 64 Barton Road was known locally as the White House. Before streets in Stretford were compulsorily numbered in 1890 the cottage was known as 'Dick Radcliffe's' after its occupier, a joiner who lived there till at least 1910. Later living there were the Daniel, Lees, Marsh, Wildsmith and Perkin families. The property has now been replaced by town houses, only its pear tree remaining.

8. *Porch House Farm*. 1271 Chester Road was a well-known landmark until it had to make way for road widening in the 1950s. Known latterly after its occupier, Arthur Pennington, its name Porch House Farm reflected its inset doorway. Not a common feature in dwelling houses, its presence can be explained by the original use of the building, it being the Pack Horse Inn from around 1714. Strings of these beasts of burden carried salt from Cheshire and textiles from Manchester along routes impassable for wheeled vehicles. Travellers halted by the Mersey floods must have been grateful for its hospitality. The fields belonging to the farm were on the other side of Chester Road, from Bradshaw Lane to the Old Cock. Grown behind the farm, rhubarb or 'Stretford Beef' was a local speciality.

9. *The Angel Hotel.* The Angel stood on Chester Road, almost opposite Chapel Lane. It was built in 1874 to replace an earlier inn and brewhouse of the same name. This inn was possibly the most important in Stretford, for as early as 1760 it was a regular stopping place for the stage coaches, which carried passengers and mail to and from Manchester. The bowling green was a magnet for some of the best bowlers in the north-west in the period between the wars. An old Stretfordian vividly remembers the tennant of a local farm, who was bowling for a cup which she had donated. Her husband's advice to her was not to back this farmer if he were sober. When he had had a drink he was unbeatable! The hotel was demolished in the early seventies for road widening.

10. *The Bishop Blaize*. The Bishop Blaize Inn was demolished in 1863 and replaced by the Talbot Hotel. One landlord lost his licence for allowing bull baiting and general unruliness. James Brindley thought over problems connected with the construction of the Bridgewater Canal whilst resting at the inn.

11. *The Talbot Hotel.* This well-known Stretford landmark, the Talbot Hotel, stood on Chester Road next to what is now the civic theatre. Built in 1863, it replaced a very old, partially thatched inn: the Bishop Blaize. The name Talbot has connections with the De Trafford family. Sir Humphrey, the 28th Lord of the Manor, married at the age of 47 Mary Annette Talbot, sister of the 17th Earl of Shrewsbury.

12. *The Old Cock Hotel.* The Old Cock Hotel in the 1870s. The name probably originates from the pastime of cock fighting which was once popular in the area.

13. *The Old Cock Inn*. This view shows the inn after its rebuilding in 1898. Its outside appearance remains unaltered to this day. The hotel was important as the terminus of horse-drawn tram services and the entrance to the stables and sheds on the right of the picture can be seen. They are still in existence and were built in 1880 on the opening of the Piccadilly-Stretford tramway.

14. *The Robin Hood Inn.* The Robin Hood Inn stood at the corner of Barton Road, then Higgin Lane, and Urmston Lane.

15. *The Robin Hood Hotel.* The inn was demolished in 1882 and replaced by the present building shown in this picture.

16. *St. Matthew's Church.* The foundation stone for St. Matthew's new church was laid by Lady De Trafford on 30th September 1841 on land previously known as Wagstaffe's Field, reputedly used for bear baiting. The dedication ceremony was performed by the Bishop of Chester on 10th October 1842. Over the century, since that dedication, changes have been made to the parish as Stretford grew in size and population and the church has continued to play an important part in Stretford life. In 1921 the south transept was made into a War Memorial Chapel dedicated to St. Martin.

17. *St. Matthew's church bells*. The new St. Matthew's Church, like its predecessor, had only one bell, used until 1863 to ring the curfew. Five more bells were provided by Mr. Henry Hayes of Myrtle Lodge, Edge Lane, in memory of his wife. These were first rung on St. Thomas' Day 1870. In 1933 they were taken down and sent back to the original foundry, John Taylor's, at Loughborough. Two new trebles were added and the eight bells rehung. This work was paid for by relatives of Alice Ada Ridge in remembrance of her long association with the church. Between the two workmen stands Walter Wigglesworth, who with his cousin David had been a bell ringer for many years. Two other families connected with the bells were the Birchalls and Wilfred Moss. In 1958 he celebrated sixty years as a bell-ringer, during which time he became a noted conductor.

18. *St. Ann's Church.* It was Sir Humphrey de Trafford who, in 1863, donated the site for St. Ann's Church on Chester Road. There had been a small chapel in Herbert Street since 1859, but this became too small for the needs of a growing community and was later used as a school. The new church was built at a cost of £24,000, the bill being met by the De Traffords. The notable Victorian architect Augustus Pugin was the designer and he followed the popular Gothic revival style of the time. Bishop Turner consecrated the church in 1867 and in the following year a fine organ was installed, made by Jardine's. The church's bene-factors, Sir Humphrey and Lady Annette de Trafford, are remembered on the right-hand side of the altar in a stained-glass window. A brass plaque and a stone carving form other tributes. The angelus bell was added in 1899.

19. *Bancroft's sweet shop*. Almost facing King Street, at 1145 Chester Road, was Bancroft's sweet shop. It was a natural calling place for generations of Stretford children. John Bancroft with his wife Cissie ran the shop in the late twenties. Their children Sid and Gertie took turns serving in the shop. Up the four stone steps for any child with a penny lay an Aladdin's cave; Devon cream toffee (cracked with the hammer), humbugs and cherry lips filled the shop with smells which so delighted the children. To the left of the shop was Madder's outdoor beer licence and on the right the Maypole grocers, with Mr. Scholes the plumber occupying the cellar premises directly under Bancroft's shop. Close by at number 1157 John's mother, Catherine, had a shop dealing in furniture.

20. *Seymour Mead's*. Seymour Mead's, grocers and provision merchants, stood on the corner of Chester Road and Newton Street. The gentleman in the doorway appears from his dress to be the manager. The right-hand window displays the 'New Fruits Strawberry Jams', and the one on the left Wiltshire and mild bacons, with hams in the centre. One is intrigued to know what is meant by 'Genuine Bacon'! Cheshire, Canadian and Gorganzola cheeses seem to be popular. Old Tawny Port is on display in the corner window. At the side a notice informs 'Perfumery', unusual for a grocer, or did it merely mean toilet soap? Records show that the shop was there from 1905.

21. *Wakefield's shop.* Situated at the corner of King Street and Chester Road this was a typical large Victorian grocer's shop, crammed with goods and provisions. Later, before final demolition, it became Raw's chemists.

22. *Robinson's shop.* Situated at the corner of Barton Road and Urmston Lane was Robinson's shop. After Robinson's of Salford left, the shop was managed by a Mr. Lunn and the picture shows him outside the shop around 1906. Later he also had a shop on Edge Lane.

23. *T. Royle and Son.* T. Royle and Son (1839-1950) were well-known grocers and provision merchants. The bakery was added in 1903. Throughout the years Royle's attained the position of the leading and largest trader of their class in the district.

24. *Chester Road, 1195-1203.* This terrace on Chester Road stood next to the Congregational Church, built in 1861. Pearsons Buildings, a small close of terraced houses, was reached by the alley on the right. Leslie Street was directly opposite. McConnell's off-licence was formerly Melross' grocer's shop while, to its left, 1197 Chester Road was Whitney's boot repairers. The bunting is probably in celebration of King George V's Silver Jubilee. Miss Hughes at 1203 rejoiced in the title of Laundry Receiving Officer.

25. *Leslie Street*. Leslie Street was off Chester Road where 'Macdonalds' now stands. Originally it was called Moore Street, after Henry Moore, whose large house at the end was Stretford's Post Office from 1870. On the left-hand side Diamond Court was a misleading name for slums equal to the worst in Manchester. The back-to-back houses had cellar dwellings below, with several families sharing the privvies. Water came from a pump. Even in Victorian times the unhealthy conditions were recognised and the area demolished. Perhaps because of the street's reputation its name was changed in 1896.

26. *Leslie Street.* This shows the wash house behind 6 Leslie Street, the furthest of the three cottages on the last photograph. In the foreground we see the boiler for Monday's washing water. Also visible is the dolly tub, made from galvanised steel, as was the small bath used to carry wet clothes to the mangle. The same family lived here for many years − in 1876 John Robinson; in 1890-1910 George Robinson, postman; and from 1928 to 1939, when it was demolished, Miss Ellen Robinson.

27. *Temperance Place.* Temperance Place was a small alley off King Street near to Church Street. The white building at the rear, the cottages and seven on King Street (later converted into shops) were reputedly built by temperance workers. Over the years the hall had many uses, concerts and Rechabite meetings. It was the first headquarters of the local Salvation Army. Eventually it became the Palace Picture House, later known as the Futurist.

28. *Bennett's Buildings*. Bennett's Buildings were situated off King Street. The terrace on King Street facing Broady Street though originally known as Bennett's Buildings was later called Dalton's Buildings. Behind ran two rows of back-to-back houses, at first numbered 9-24 but later given the numbers 1-16. The photo shows the rear of Dalton's Buildings and 1-8 Bennett's Buildings. At the end of the close is the communal toilet block, with the Methodist Church behind. The Lancashire actor John Comer, well-known for the portrayal of the café owner in the series 'Last of the Summer Wine' was born in one of the houses on the left.

29. Numbers 9-16 Bennett's Buildings (more commonly known as Bennett's Bugs) were built onto the backs of numbers 1-8. To each house entry was by a single door.

30. *Pinnington Lane.* At a time when Pinnington Lane really was a country lane, in the 1850s, a small block of houses was built at the corner of King Street opposite the old police station. This was Twyford Place, built to a design that was commonplace at that period of two rows of back-to-back houses with a paved yard in between them. Lack of essential amenities led to these houses being declared unfit and they were demolished in the 1930s.

31. *Stretford Police Station.* Situated at the corner of Pinnington Lane and King Street the station is also shown on another photograph of King Street. It was opened in 1897, closed in 1954 and was finally demolished in 1968.

32. *The Pinfold.* The Pinfold at the corner of Barton Road and King Street was used to hold stray animals which could be a nuisance on the roads. The animals could be recovered by their owners on payment of a fine. Cock-fighting also took place occasionally in the pinfold. It was removed in 1905.

Pinfold Farm. 'Another Danger Spot near City' and 'Daily Shocks for Residents' were headlines in the Evening Chronicle in July 1929. They referred to the junction of Barton Road and King Street, on one corner of which stood Pinfold Farm. The picturesque thatched farmhouse was built in the days when Stretford was a farming community. The country lanes had by 1929 become busy roads, with a stream of traffic to and from Trafford Park. In an attempt to prevent more accidents, the Council ordered broad white lines and 'Danger' to be painted on the road. Pinfold Court commemorates the name of the farm demolished in 1939.

33. *The Fowt Barton Road.* The group of cottages at the corner of Barton Road and Chapel Lane on the site now covered by Stretford House, was officially known as Bradshaw Fold, though many people called it t'Fowt, possibly a corruption of Fold. It was a small community several of whose members were connected with market gardening. In the 1920s Thomas Price lived at No. 50 Barton Road, the cottage facing the road, and Thomas Richardson lived at No. 44, the middle cottage in the Fold. Both were market gardeners. For many years during the 1920s and 30s the small cottage next to John Richardson was inhabited by Frank Otwell, a coach painter. At Nos. 46-48, at the far end beyond the white gate, lived John Howarth and his family who for many years ran a nursery and market garden there. John Howarth's wife, formerly Bridget O'Mara, came from Ireland to enter domestic service. To her employers she was 'Ellen' to distinguish her from a Bridget already employed.

34. *Chester Road.* This view of Chester Road taken in 1870, shows how it looked at the turn of the century with the pattern of twentieth century Stretford beginning to emerge. Edge Lane runs off to the right by the shop.

35. *Trafford View.* 753-7 Chester Road stood in the Great Stone district, in a position now opposite Ravenswood Road. The gable at the left was Mona Villa, facing Clyne House. Built before 1840, the block was L-shaped; six back-to-back houses at right angles were later knocked through, known as Trafford View. In the late 1920s Mrs. Bleakley ran the shop which had earlier been run for many years by Mr. Jesse Adams. The sign advertises a product of the Palatine Bottling Company's Imperial Brewery of Birch Street, West Gorton.

36. *Derbyshire Lane*. This photograph taken around 1900, shows Derbyshire Lane looking towards Chester Road. Moss Road is on the left and Pinnington Lane on the right. The picture emphasises the rural nature of Stretford before rapid industrialisation.

37. *King Street.* The photograph about 1890 gives a good impression of the street. On the left is part of Wakefield's shop and on the right the butcher at the corner later became the Picturedrome cinema.

38. The second picture of the street shows it decorated for the Coronation of Edward VII in 1902. The view is towards Chester Road. On the left is the police station, opened in 1897. The street did not change substantially until the extensive redevelopment of the 1960s.

39. The third photograph shows the contrasts along King Street with the girls walking in front of Vine House covered in grape vine. Vine house existed with modifications until 1965.

40. *Edge Lane*. This picture taken about 1900, shows a more leisurely age.

41. *Stretford Station.* Users of Metrolink today will readily recognise the Stretford station building of the 1900s, as the site of the present building is the same and it is about the same size as the old. This served the Manchester South Junction and Altrincham Railway, opened in 1849, from Manchester London Road to Altrincham. Note the horse-drawn bus linking Stretford and Urmston stations.

42. *Edge Lane*. The stretch of Edge Lane from Chester road towards the station is shown here. Stretford's coaling wharf lay behind the terrace and served the canal and the railway for the transhipment of goods.

43. *Trafford Bar*. Situated at the Manchester end of Talbot Road it was on the Stretford-Manchester turn-pike. Three other tolls were at Crossford Bridge, Longford and Cornbrook. Tolls were abolished in 1885. The Toll Bar is commemorated in the name of the public house near the site shown in the photograph.

44. *Stamford Street, Old Trafford.* This picture was taken about 1900. Stamford Street was one of a number of streets of similar appearance in the area. Old Trafford developed rapidly in the 1800s and was distinct from Stretford 'village'. It was more closely linked to Manchester. The subsequent development of Gorse Hill and Firswood served to link Old Trafford to Stretford, although considerable rivalry existed between the north and south of the district.

45. *Chester Road, White City.* Taken in 1905 the picture shows Chester Road near Henshaw's School for the Blind. The school is on the left.

46. *Lewis' coach 1892*. The photograph was taken by Frank Hulme, 1070 Chester Road. The coach ran between Manchester and Liverpool and photographs taken by Frank Hulme in the morning were ready to sell to passengers on the return trip in the evening.

47. *Cottages on Pool Lane.* Pool Lane became Market Street and curved from Brunswick Street to King Street. This view about 1890 contrasts the old cottages with 'modern' Victorian terraces.

48. *Cobb Hall cottages*. The cottages, part of Cob Hall Farm, were situated where Stretford house now stands and shows once more the village atmosphere of old Stretford.

49. *The last load of hay*. Gaushill Farm became Gorse Hill and was the start of 'ribbon' development in the area between about 1895 to 1905. The last load of hay leaves a field at Gorse Hill and marks the demise of rural Stretford. New housing is evident in the background.

50. *Clyne House*. Clyne House was built as a private residence. Later it was taken over by the Royal Schools for the Deaf.

51. *The Civic Theatre*. The Civic Theatre was built by John Rylands in 1878. It had lecture rooms and a free lending library. After his death it was bought by the Local Board, the forerunner of the local authority. Old Trafford objected to public offices at the 'village' and as a result Trafford Public Hall was built on Talbot Road in 1889.

52. *Trafford Old Hall.* This was situated on the Boyer Street side of Chester Road next to the railway cutting which passes under Boyer Street and Talbot Road. It was taken down in 1939.

53. *The Picturedrome.* The first purpose-built cinema in Stretford occupied the corner of King Street and Chester Road. In the 1920s 'talkies' replaced the silent films watched to the accompaniment of appropriate piano music. An important part of Stretford social life, it fell to the developers in the 1960s.

54. *The electricity station*. Opened in October 1903 the station was situated near Longford Bridge at a cost of 35,000 pounds and was an important stage in the modern development of Stretford, allowing the gradual replacement of the well-established gas lighting for public and domestic use.

55. *Westinghouse.* Trafford Park Estates was established in 1896 and in 1899 the American company Westinghouse came to the park. Part of the original team is shown in the picture.

56. The firm quickly became a large employer being able to exploit the excellent water and rail transport facilities nearby. The company became, in turn, Metropolitan Vicker's, A.E.I., G.E.C., and finally G.E.C.-Alsthom. How quickly the firm developed is shown in this impressive photograph taken as early as 1905.

57. *Trafford Park Industrial Estate.* The Bridgewater Canal cut across several roads in Stretford. One road, Old Lane, later Moss Lane, led to Trafford Hall and Trafford Park Farm and it was necessary to provide a bridge over the canal. Taylor's bridge became Moss Lane Bridge and was continually widened and strengthened as it became one of the entrances to Metropolitan Vicker's, now G.E.C.-Alsthom. The tower, shown in the photograph, was used to support the aerials for one of the first radio stations in the country, 2ZY.

58. The interior of the station is also shown.

59. *Steam road roller*. This machine made by Aveling and Porter was widely used in making the improved roads required by increasing traffic in the 1900s. They were familiar sights on the roads for many years.

60. *A horse-drawn tram.* This photograph was taken at the Old Cock where the horses were changed and the tram switched tracks for the return journey. The body swung round on the chassis to facilitate change of direction. Horses were used for about three hours per day and had a working life of about four years.

61. *The last tram Chester Road.* Taken on 6th June 1931, when the last trams ran through Stretford, this standard bogie car with hard wooden seating is heading out to Sale Moor on route 49. Electric trams replaced horse-drawn trams in April 1903, when routes 47 and 48 ran to the Old Cock. These were extended in stages until a service to Altrincham was started in 1907. The tram hides the window of Seymour Mead's, but from the left are the shops of James Harrop and Son, tailors; Samuel Broadbent, chemist; Thomas Stephenson, photographer; and Burston and Nixon, grocers.

62. *The Bridgewater Canal.* The original route of the Duke of Bridgewater's canal from Worsley to Manchester was on the Salford side of the Irwell. During construction, permission was obtained to re-route it via an aqueduct over the Irwell to Stretford and thence to Manchester. When the canal had reached Stretford in 1761 the Duke decided to extend it 24 miles to Runcorn to capture some of the Liverpool trade. The junction of the Worsley to Manchester Canal with the Runcorn extension is the Bridgewater Junction, but locally it is known as Waters Meetings. As the route of the extension brought the canal to the centre of Stretford, it not only enabled coal to be bought more cheaply, but also provided a relatively quick and cheap route for passengers. The building on the left was perhaps a toll house and the bridge a continuation of the towpath.

63. *Trafford Hall.* Wickleswick Hall was bought by Sir Cecil de Trafford in 1635. Trafford Hall was built on the site and occupied by the family until 1896, when the site was sold to Trafford Park Estates. It was used as a prisoner-of-war camp in the First World War.

64. *Longford Park*. The open spaces of Longford Park were bought for the people of Stretford in 1911. With the absorption of so many fields for housing, it offered a welcome change of scenery and recreation.

65. *Longford Hall*. The hall, built in 1857, was the home of John Rylands, a wealthy textile manufacturer and philanthropist. He is now remembered in the name of the internationally famous John Rylands Library in Manchester, built by his third wife. He died at the hall in 1888 and his wife lived there into this century. After it passed to Stretford, the hall was used among other purposes for civic functions, art exhibitions and, perhaps best remembered, for local society and church dances. Also noteworthy were the firework displays at the annual pageants.

STRETFORD ROSE QUEEN FESTIVAL 1913.
PHOTO:-A.M.Lloyd,

66. *Pageant festivities*. The pageant has been an annual event from at least the 1800s and is still held today. In the past it acquired a reputation for riotous and drunken disorder. Local transport of the time was used for the various decorated floats.

67. This picture, as the previous one taken in 1913, captures the atmosphere of the pageant and shows the horse-drawn transport of the time.

68. *Char-à-banc trip*. Char-à-banc trips were very popular in the 1920s. Although slow, open to the elements and bumpy (note the solid tyres) they are fondly remembered. Here a party from St. Matthew's arrives for a day out in Derbyshire. The ever present Walter Wigglesworth seems to be in charge.

69. *Gorse Hill School Prize Day*. 'An occasion unique in the history of Stretford' was how the local paper reported an event at Gorse Hill School in December 1920. This was the opening of the first rate-aided school library in Stretford. A collection of 400 books chosen by the chief librarian was established at Gorse Hill, because that school was farthest away from any of the public libraries. The opening ceremony was performed by Councillor J.W. Dorran, Chairman of the Libraries committee, who hoped to see libraries in every school as soon as possible. The photograph shows Councillor Dorran presenting prizes to the pupils at the school in 1926.

70. *Stretford Girls' High School.* In 1922 the girls moved from Old Trâfford to premises at Heath House, near Great Stone Road. This building, which had been an orphanage, became Stretford High School. Numbers increased and extensive new premises were opened in 1927. The old house was still used as an office, staff room and headmistress's study and the sixth form still inhabited the attics. The school was bombed in 1940 and after some years at Gorse Park the school moved to new premises off Edge Lane in 1954.

71. *Victoria Park Infant School.* Victoria Park Infant School, opened in 1914, was built to the newest design of the Board of Education as a corridor school. Shortly after opening it was requisitioned as a military hospital and the children were accommodated in Sunday Schools until the end of the war. This photograph taken about 1926, shows a typical classroom, with a dado of green-glazed brick round the wall and rows of dual desks each with inkwell and neatly placed paper. Through the window can be seen the enclosed corridor, with pictures on the walls. Beneath the window were display cases opening onto the corridor.

BONTOG IGORROTE'S SPEAR THROWING AT THE WHITE CITY.
PROF PALMER'S SERIES.

72. *The White City.* The photograph was taken at the opening of the entertainments centre in 1907 after the closure and subsequent sale of the Botanical Gardens. Apparently a display of spear throwing was a feature of the opening of the short-lived entertainment centre. A water shute seen in the background was a feature of the centre.

73. Later, greyhound racing was well established here. Today the original gates are retained as a focal point of the modern shopping development.

74. *The Royal Jubilee Exhibition.* This was held in 1887 on the south side of the Botanical Gardens, where the White City development now stands. It was a shop window for Manchester enterprise as confidence and pride in the city was at a low ebb.

75. Photograph 74 and this one give a good impression of the scale of the exhibition which was a great success. With the decline in popularity of the gardens and the expense of upkeep the structures were demolished at the turn of the century.

Streitford.

Big Stone Cottages.

November 9th 190

The Wrench Series. No. 2815.

76. *Big Stone Cottages*. These cottages were situated close to the corner of Chester Road and Great Stone Road. They took their name from the 'Big Stone', which lay at one time inside the railings on the right of the picture.